Medals *Above My* Heart

The Rewards of Being a Military Wife

Medals *Above* *My* Heart

The Rewards of Being a Military Wife

BRENDA PACE
CAROL MCGLOTHLIN

BROADMAN
& HOLMAN
PUBLISHERS

Nashville, Tennessee

Medals Above My Heart
Copyright © 2004 by Brenda Pace and Carol McGlothlin
All rights reserved

ISBN: 0-8054-3184-5

Broadman and Holman Publishers
Nashville, Tennessee
www.broadmanholman.com

Unless otherwise noted, all Scripture quotations
are from the Holy Bible, New International Version.
Copyright © 1973, 1978, 1984 by International Bible Society.
Used by permission of Zondervan Bible Publishers.

Scriptures marked (NASB) are taken from
the New American Standard Bible®, Copyright ©
1960,1962,1963,1968,1971,1972,1973,1975,1977,1995
by The Lockman Foundation. Used by permission.

Dewey Decimal Classification: 242.643
Subject Heading: Devotional Literature / Military Personnel / Wives

Printed in Korea
1 2 3 4 07 06 05 04

Dedication

This book is dedicated to every military wife who has chosen to follow her military man . . . wherever that may be.

Where you go I will go,
and where you stay I will stay.
—Ruth 1:16

Table of Contents

Medal of Honor 11

1. Basic Training 12
2. 100% ID Check 16
3. Leave and Cleave 19
4. Say What? 23
5. My Typical Life 26
6. Follow Me 30
7. Sensory Memories 33
8. Beacons of Hope 37

Purple Heart 41

9. Drippy, Dark Sin 42
10. Packing Up 46
11. Door to Door 49
12. Attack on the Comfort Zone 52
13. A Hidden Gem 55
14. Up in Smoke 59
15. Pray for Your Children 62
16. A Porcelain Box and Trouser Socks 66

Bronze Star .69

17. My Father's Hand 70

18. When It All Comes Crashing Down 73

19. Hurry Up and Wait 76

20. D-Day 79

21. Timing 83

22. Fear Factor 86

23. Back to the Desert 90

24. Life in 3D 94

Distinguished Service Award . . .99

25. Boots over the Wire 100

26. Support and Exhort 103

27. Red and Yellow, Black and White 106

28. Clinging to the Vine 109

29. Training for the Real World 112

30. Where Now? 116

31. How Does That Translate? 120

32. Looking Ahead 123

Preface

A woman who fears the Lord is to be praised.
Give her the reward she has earned.

—Proverbs 31:30-31

Medals are received for accomplishments, and they become symbols of experiences. They display the history of any member of the Armed Forces—soldier, airman, marine, coastguardsman, or sailor. One can view the uniform of someone in the military and know where they have been and what they have done.

Our husbands wear their medals on their uniforms. In this book—as we share some experiences of military life—we will reveal the medals we wear over our own hearts.

Every military wife has a story to tell, and the legacy of those military wives who have gone before us will always be remembered in history. From Martha Washington, Libby Custer, and Mamie Eisenhower to their present-day successors, military wives have always experienced challenges that have stretched their physical, emotional, and spiritual resources.

While it is an honor to serve with our husbands as they defend the freedom we enjoy as Americans, our service by their side is not without sacrifice. There are no military service medals that are handed out to military wives for their bravery, gallantry, heroism, or exceptional service. The rewards, however, are greater than any medal could display. The life of the military wife is one that reaps exceptional benefits through personal character and leadership development, adventure, relationships, and opportunities for service.

Uncertain times, though, make a military wife's need for encouragement crucial. The new, unconventional type of warfare we are experiencing today, for example, brings with it great insecurities and fear of the unknown. And while we are of the opinion that the military life is exceptional, there are times when a woman associated with the military is left feeling vulnerable and in need of understanding. A desire to connect and be comforted is of utmost importance.

Our prayer is that through this inspirational collection of devotions gleaned from our own experiences as military wives, you will see God's hand at work in and through your own life.

We pray that you will laugh and cry as you are reminded of the many times you have been in situations such as those shared in this book. As you read each entry, may you realize the privilege and honor it is to be a part of the military culture.

As you read the Scriptures, may you be encouraged to see the practicality and personal application of God's Word in the everyday happenings of military life.

And as you pray the prayers at the end of each entry, may you recognize the joy of trusting Him to use the unique experiences military life brings to develop you into the woman of God He desires you to be.

—*Carol and Brenda*

Medal of Honor

Given for exceptional gallantry in action

A young wife can feel overwhelmed when thrust into the military world. Not only may her personal identity feel threatened as she becomes known as a "dependent," but the learning curve is steep as she learns the traditions, lingo, and overall culture of the military. The joys can be many, however, as she discovers the rich and noble heritage she has entered. Indeed, there are *Medals of Honor* available for the woman who becomes involved and active in her military community.

Basic Training

I remember my first real experience as a new military wife. The year was 1974. I had been a military wife for only one month when my husband, Richard, brought an invitation home, requesting my presence at the Commanding General's house to meet his wife. The bottom corner of the invitation read, "R.S.V.P. (hats and gloves required)."

Well, in my 1970s "I am woman, hear me roar" attitude, I must admit I felt somewhat rebellious at the thought of someone telling me what I was supposed to wear. I did as I was instructed, however, and showed up in full attire.

It wasn't until then that I understood. As I waited in line to be greeted by the General's wife, I realized what a noble and respectful life I had just entered. Most of us were more dressed up than we would have been to attend a church service. We were in true lady's attire, and it commanded a lady's attitude. Our dress and preparation also commanded respect for the General's position of leadership and the lady we had come there to meet.

Looking back on that day thirty years ago, it's clear that the times have certainly changed. The tradition is not quite as strong anymore, and the dress requirements are a bit more casual. The respect and honor are still there, whether it be "hat and gloves required" or Sunday attire. The heart is the true test of appearance.

I have often thought about that experience, marveling at how it compares to my daily walk with Jesus. How much time do I actually take in preparing to meet Him and honor Him each day? The less time I spend, the less prepared I am to honor Him. Yet the more time I spend each day in reading the Word and praying, the more time He gives me not only to honor Him but also to be honorable for Him.

How do we prepare to "dress" each day to meet the One who both created and commands the universe? How do we honor and greet the One who has loved us and known us even before we were knit together in our mother's womb?

—Carol

Finally, brethren, whatever is true, whatever is honorable, whatever is right, whatever is pure, whatever is lovely, whatever is of good repute, if there is any excellence and if anything worthy of praise, let your mind dwell on these things. The things you have learned and received and heard and seen in me, practice these things; and the God of peace shall be with you.
—Philippians 4:8-9 (NASB)

Precious Lord, thank You for the time You give me in my day to prepare to serve You. Thank You for the privilege You have given me to communicate with You through prayer and Your Word. Lord, I pray that You would make me honorable and true and lovely in Your sight from the inside out. You are worthy of all respect and honor and glory. In Jesus' name. Amen.

100% ID Check

$\mathcal{I}$ am a card-carrying military wife. The card of which I speak, of course, is my military ID card. It is a card I definitely "don't leave home without."

Listed on this card are my soldier husband's name, rank, and serial number. Upon closer inspection one can also decipher my relationship to him—"SP"—(I assume this is an abbreviation for "spouse"), the date of expiration, and the listing of the privileges this card affords me.

Each time I enter a military installation, I am required to produce this card and have my obligatory, unflattering picture inspected. After a thorough examination to confirm that the picture and my face are indeed a match, I am offered a "have a nice day, ma'am" and ushered through the gates.

A person only has to lose or misplace a military ID card once to realize the importance of taking good care of this little plastic-coated certificate. It is the official ticket for entry to any military facility, an absolute necessity for everything from shopping to medical attention.

There are those who actually resent this identification process. I've never been able to understand this attitude. To me, this card is tangible proof that I belong. I am privileged to drive through the gates and gain access to places that those who are non-ID card holders cannot. The card clearly states on the front that it is my "Identification and Privilege Card."

While I do not resent having to carry my military ID card, I am grateful that when I come to God in prayer, I do not have to flash an ID card to receive access to Him. John 10:14-15 describes Jesus as One who identifies His own people with a supernatural identification. Jesus stated, "I am the good shepherd; I know my sheep and my sheep know me—just as the Father knows me and I know the Father."

Yes, He knows me fully, as written in 1 Corinthians 13:12: "Now we see but a poor reflection as in a mirror; then we shall see face to face. Now I know in part; then I shall know fully, even as I am fully known."

Won't that be a wonderful day when we are ushered into heavenly gates? There will be no flash of a card, because we are fully known by our Lord.

—Brenda

Father, thank You for the privilege of being identified as Your own. May I live this day reflecting You and identifying You to a world that desperately needs to see Your face. I look forward to the day when You will usher me into the heavenly Kingdom to live and reign with You forever! Amen.

Leave and Cleave

If you want to experience the truth of Genesis 2:24 (NASB)—"For this cause [the covenant of marriage] a man shall leave his father and his mother, and shall cleave to his wife"—just marry a soldier, sailor, airman, coast-guardsman, or marine. You will then understand to the fullest just what God had in mind when He gave this instruction!

Like me, most of you had already lived away from home by the time you married, whether it was because of college or a job. When you marry a military man, however, leaving home may not only mean moving to another town but possibly another country! Military orders are always just around the corner, although they can take you clear around the world. And while this can bring much angst for the new military wife, it can also drive a military couple to depend more upon each other.

This became especially true for my husband and me (Carol) when after only nine months of marriage, he received orders to report to Germany. I remember driving to Charleston, South Carolina, thinking (as my parents followed us in a car close behind), "This is it. I will never see my parents or family again." I had known Richard for a very long time, but it became very real to me that he was going to be all I had from this point on. I was leaving behind everything else I held dear in my life to travel halfway around the world. Would the love we had for each other be strong enough to withstand this adjustment?

They say, "All you need is love." And in a sense this is true—as long as it is God's love, not merely the natural, human kind. The world defines love as a mysterious feeling a person falls into—and out of—at the whim of fate. But the Bible is woven with the thread of true love from beginning to end. Within its covers we learn that true love is defined as passion anchored by commitment.

At the wedding of their son recently, Brenda's husband, Richard, used a wonderful story to illustrate this concept. He asked the congregation to imagine a kite in the shape of a heart (representing our passion in a relationship) attached to a string (representing our commitment). Just as a kite dances in the breeze, the passion of true love desires to dance in the winds of life and relationship. Some may think the string of commitment holds this passion

back, but in fact it is just the opposite. If you cut the string from a kite, it may momentarily look as though it has sprung free to experience new flight. But if you follow it long enough, you'll eventually find the kite tangled in a tree or broken on the ground.

To fly higher, a kite does not need to be cut free; it just needs more string. The greater the cord of commitment in a marriage, the higher the passions can fly. When you become skilled in true love, knowing how to balance both commitment and passion, your kite will dance in the winds of love, free to soar and turn loops, knowing the string of commitment will keep it safe.

Upon reflection I see I was being slightly overdramatic in those early years when I thought I would never see my family again. The fact is, the military forced us to leave home and family, yet this transition actually helped us choose to cleave to one another. I am grateful that as a result of this choice, our commitment to one another—and our love for one another—has been solidified and strengthened.

Jesus stated in Mark 12:30-31 that the greatest commandment is to "Love the Lord your God with all your heart and with all your soul and with all your mind and with all your strength. The second is this: 'Love your neighbor as yourself.'" Would it not be safe to say that your closest neighbor is your spouse?

The charge given by Chaplain Pace at the close of the wedding ceremony reflected the unique blessings of a Jesus-centered marriage. He said, "My grandmother passed on the secret of marital success to my bride and me when we were married twenty-nine years ago, and today I pass it on to you. She told me that if we both lived first for the Lord and then lived for each other instead of for ourselves, we would have a happy marriage. Her words were not as eloquent as the Lord's in Mark 12:31, but she spoke with the confidence of experience that this truth from the Word of God works in marriage."

I can only add to that: "Amen!"

— Carol and Brenda

Father, thank You for my husband and the blessing he is to me. I am grateful that You have allowed us to join in the covenant relationship of marriage. Help me to be the best neighbor to him that I can be. Allow our marriage to be characterized by passion anchored with commitment. May the love we have for each other be greater as a result of the love we have for You. Amen.

Say What?

"Can I meet you at the ACS to find out about the TDY and PCS instructions?"

Ah, the joy of acronyms! The military has certainly cornered the market on this literary application.

During our first year of military life, Richard brought home a ten-page list of acronyms that he said would help me communicate when I spoke with people. I knew there was no way I would ever learn these on my own. I was quite sure, in fact, that I would forever carry this ten-page list with me as if it were a foreign language dictionary. I could see myself politely holding my hand up and saying, "Just one moment, let me look that up," as I thumbed through the pages.

As a new wife in the military, for instance, you might get a flier that reads: "Meeting at the PX for the ACS staff to discuss PCS moves and TDY separations. You will need your LES and your ETS if that applies. Open to all OWC, NCOWC, PWOC, MCCW participants."

My first response to this, before becoming indoctrinated in military culture, would have been: "What planet are you from? Get me back to the real world!" But I was amazed how easily I began to speak the lingo as it became a daily part of my life. The acronyms just flowed from my mouth. I could not imagine any other way of communicating.

Upon my husband's retirement, we filtered more and more into the civilian world. I continued for a while to use my military lingo with civilian friends and found myself faced with puzzled looks. The language that was so natural to me was truly "Greek" to them.

But actually—whether it is corporate America, the education system, homemaking, or the military—each institution has its own jargon. Being able to speak the language of some particular field gives one a sense of belonging. It is difficult for me to describe the joy I felt in belonging to the military family, able to deal comfortably with their way of speaking. It was a niche that fit me well, one I got used to.

This joy, however, is nothing compared to the joy I feel in being a part of the family of God. Ephesians 2:19-22 says it this way: "You are no longer foreigners and aliens, but fellow citizens with God's people and members of God's household, built on the foundation of the apostles and prophets, with Christ Jesus himself as the chief cornerstone. In him the whole building is joined together and rises to become a holy temple in the Lord. And in him you too are being built together to become a dwelling in which God lives by his Spirit."

In other words, while I am on TDY, I am to find my MOS so I can fit into the UMT to prepare for our PCS.

Is that a puzzled look on your face?

—*Carol*

"I have put my words in your mouth and covered
you with the shadow of my hand——I who set the
heavens in place, who laid the foundations of the
earth, and who say to Zion, 'You are my people.'"

—Isaiah 51:16

*Father God, Creator, Completer of the universe, You are the only
thing that matters in this world. Thank You for giving me the confidence that I belong to You — "accepted in the Beloved." I am Your
child and a part of Your Body. May I speak the language of Your
love today. May my words encourage and bless others. May I be
actively involved in building Your kingdom and helping others
know what it means to belong to You. In Jesus' name. Amen.*

Acronym Index
PX—Post Exchange
ACS—Army Community Service
TDY—Temporary Duty
LES—Leave and Earning Statement
ETS—Estimated Time of Separation
OWC—Officers Wives Club
NCOWC—Non-Commissioned Officers Wives Club
PWOC—Protestant Women of the Chapel
MCCW—Military Council of Catholic Women
MOS—Military Occupation Specialty
UMT—Unit Ministry Team
PCS—Permanent Change of Station

My Typical Life

"A typical little preacher's wife,"
my friends in college told me.
    They all had my future planned,
the course I'd come to see.
    But something about that word
"typical" just went against my
grain;
    I wanted my life to be unique, not
the familiar old refrain!
    I'd see the world—backpack for
Jesus, and sing to all the masses,
    Not be stuck in some po-dunk
church where life moved slow as
molasses!

As an immature college student, this was my take on a future as a minister's wife. I longed for adventure and new experiences. I had been born in a small Southern town that was home to our denominational headquarters. I was raised in a minister's home and wanted to do something different! The last thing I wanted to be was "typical." (Webster defines typical as "constituting or having the nature of a type; conforming to what is expected in the ordinary course of events.")

But I married that preacher, and we went to that po-dunk church in Georgia. The people there called me "Sister Pace," and for the longest time I kept looking around trying to see when my mother-in-law had walked in the door. Our first child, Gregory, was born in this typical Southern town, and I have recollections of these very loving people opening their arms to us. Isn't that "typical" of God's people?

After two years Richard felt an urge to do something not typical for a Southern boy. He felt a burden to pastor in the Midwest, which set us on our way to become "missionaries to Minnesota!" We answered that call and began an adventure that holds priceless memories. It was there that I became the official "pastor's wife." A congregation of dear people accepted a very young and inexperienced couple right where we were. I was never made to feel like I was too young, and they even seemed proud and happy to call us Pastor and Sister Pace. (By then, I had to get used to it; my mother-in-law was a thousand miles away!)

We were there to serve. God had called us and enabled us to do the job. The confidence these people placed in us was amazing. I see now, though, that it was not confidence in us but an unwavering confidence in God that His work would be done. Again—so "typical" of God's people!

I got used to the typical preacher's wife role and liked it. In fact, I was ready to plant myself there for good to raise my boys. There was something very special about the

Midwestern mind-set. I was content.

It was then, however, that my husband received a call from our denomination that Uncle Sam wanted him. So in May of that year, we said good-bye to our lovely congregation and headed to Fort Benning, Georgia.

One cannot describe military life as typical. It is more atypical. All of Richard's assignments have been different. The neighbors and people we have met are different. The experiences and situations have all been different.

So everything I dreamed of as a young person has all culminated in this military lifestyle. I have more than seen the world; I have lived on each side of it. I have sung to the masses—basic trainees in camouflage fatigues who said "hooah" instead of "amen" and gave a whole new meaning to making a "joyful noise to the Lord!"

God was preparing me in those first loving churches, helping me see that when we are in His perfect will, doing the work He has called us to do, the only thing typical will be His faithfulness!

The Greek word for "faithfulness" is *emunah*, which carries with it the meaning of "certainty." It expresses an assurance of God's covenant relationship with us. And because of this assurance, I have come to appreciate from the Lord's perspective what could be described as His "typical" relationship with us, which is one where He's consistent, faithful, and certain toward us.

That preacher's wife I did become,
But life's been all but typical.
The wonders of the world I've seen;
I think it's just a miracle
How God can take our heart's desires,
And in His time and will,
Bring them to pass as we delight in Him
And let us His Spirit fill.

—Brenda

Because of the Lord's great love we are not consumed, for his compassions never fail. They are new every morning; great is your faithfulness.
—Lamentations 3:22-23

Faithful Father, thank You for allowing me to be in covenant relationship with You. You have proven Yourself to be faithful in my life over and over again. There is comfort in knowing that I can be a "typical" child of God—one who knows with certainty that I belong to You. May I be aware today of Your constant presence in my life. Use me to bless others today and make Your presence known in my home and my community. Amen.

Follow Me

There was a time when I was in the habit of going in to work with my husband at "0-dark thirty." He would have his quiet time in his office while I went to exercise in the gym. An hour later we switched places, and he did PT (physical training) with the other soldiers while I had my quiet time. We would then go home and get ready for the day ahead with these most important things accomplished. It was a great plan for us for a season.

The office Richard occupied sat on Ardennes Street in Fort Bragg, North Carolina. The very mention of the name of this street brings a look of pride on any paratrooper's face. The memory of 82nd Airborne soldiers jumping into the Ardennes Forest in France for "Operation Market Garden" is revered and honored.

Several mornings a week, I was startled out of my early morning quiet time with a choir of soldiers running down the street. The choir was led by a sergeant singing out "jodies" (or cadence calls) in a strong and loud voice. These rhythmic messages enable the soldiers to keep time as they run.

You might think that this would be very distracting, especially while I was reading the Word of God and praying. Remarkably, though, this was not the case. For me, there was something very comforting about the unified voices following the confident leader.

My mind wandered to the fact that even this small act of leading and following is great in the broad scheme of things. These soldiers are trained to follow their leaders into battle. They work together to build a force of unified action and purpose.

Leader: I don't know but I've been told . . .

Echo: I don't know but I've been told . . .

Leader: I'm gonna walk on streets of gold.

Echo: I'm gonna walk on streets of gold.

Leader: If I follow where He leads . . .

Echo: If I follow where He leads . . .

Leader: A home in heaven waits for me.

Echo: A home in heaven waits for me.

What voices will you follow today? Will you follow the voices of those who will lead you into erroneous thoughts and actions? Or will you listen to the voice of the One who will lead you into all truth?

—Brenda

"My sheep listen to my voice; I know them, and they follow me."

—John 10:27

Great Shepherd, open my ears to hear Your voice today. As I am bombarded with voices shouting directions that would lead me astray, help me to follow the voice of truth. Let me echo what I have heard in Your Word to a world that is desperate for integrity. I also pray for our national leaders today. May they be men and women who look to You for guidance and lead our nation with honor, integrity, and godly wisdom. Amen.

Sensory Memories

Have you ever thought about what a gift our senses are? Seeing, smelling, tasting, touching, and hearing are all gifts from God. If you have never thought about this precious part of Creation, meet with someone who is missing one of these.

We have a dear friend who has lost her hearing. She has lights that blink when the phone or doorbell rings. She writes her communication with people through the TDD (Telecommunications Device for the Deaf) or pen and paper. Her youngest granddaughter is a singing performer, and she will never physically hear her sing again.

There are so many things in the military that alert our senses. I remember hearing, as Brenda mentioned earlier, the cadence of physical training in the early hours of the morning. I remember the constant sounds of helicopters overhead at Fort Rucker, Alabama, reminding me daily of the never-ending preparation to defend. I cannot forget the smells of the German bakeries, guesthouses cooking schnitzel, or street stands cooking bratwurst. Korean kimshee and fresh fish markets will stay in my memory forever. I recall with fondness the historical sights and beauty of places like Fort Leavenworth, Kansas.

I remember hugging Richard in the mornings before he was off to work—the smell of aftershave on his face and the crunchy feel of his freshly starched BDUs (Battle Dress Uniform). I can close my eyes and see the parade field as soldiers marched by with the flag flying high, backed by the sound of the Army band. What emotions these memories still bring to mind, especially during this time of war and unrest in the world.

There are other sounds I remember, as well—sounds of freedom and sounds of danger. While in Korea, we lived close to one of the gates that surrounded the housing owned by the American Embassy. Each time I heard a "blink blink," I knew cars were crossing over the steel rod that would close the gates in case of an attack. It was a comforting sound to me.

We also experienced the sounds of loud drums each spring, as the Korean college students protested against Americans being stationed in South Korea. It was a sort of spring break rebellion. I also remember the sound of the cannon going off every night at 5:00 p.m. at Fort Leavenworth, quickly followed by the national anthem being played. There was no greater comfort than to see the honor shown in those few minutes, as everyone paused and either saluted in uniform or stopped the car and got out, their right hands clasped to their hearts. Even young people on the fields playing soccer, football, and baseball would stop with hands over hearts to hear freedom's sound.

We are blessed to have our God-given senses to make us aware of the legacy and sacrifices that have gone before us, as well as those that will continue on after we are gone.

At the time of this writing, President George W. Bush is President and Commander-in-Chief of the United States. Military men and women salute him as he walks by and turn toward him with the salute and body movement as a show of honor to him. I witnessed it for myself on the news one night as they showed the president emerging from his helicopter after arriving at the White House from Camp David.

Having keen senses to see such stirring, patriotic sights, and being aware of everything that goes on around us in our world, is something we should never take for granted.

As you go out today on your daily walk with Him, take the time to be aware of all the sights, smells, sounds, and tastes that surround you. Ask the Lord to make you conscious of all of them. Whenever you think there isn't anything to be thankful for, sense His presence with your senses!

—*Carol*

No eye has seen, no ear has heard,
no mind has conceived what God has prepared
for those who love him.

—1 Corinthians 2:9

Thank You, Lord, for all the things around us that we are able to enjoy and experience through the gift of our senses. How enriching and amazing is your glory in all the earth! Amen.

Beacons of Hope

𝔍 do not take lightly the privilege our nation affords us to gather each week in a military chapel. I see these buildings as beacons of hope on military installations around the world. I take it even further and declare that my worship in a military chapel on a weekly basis becomes a link to a national consciousness of God. As people gather in a military chapel as part of an expression of a personal relationship with Jesus, they are participating in something that I acknowledge as amazing.

The military chapel is recognized as a part of the government structure. Yet the faith that we come there to proclaim is not a national or a state faith. It is a collective gathering of people who have a personal faith in Christ.

There are those in our society who think we should

remove all forms of religion from federal property; the chapel doors should be locked; the Bibles removed from the pews; the hymns of faith no longer sung. But as long as the Lord and the law afford us the privilege, the message of Christ needs to be proclaimed in military chapels.

As long as there are soldiers who want faith in their foxholes, the message of Christ needs to be proclaimed in military chapels.

As long as there are airmen who want to mount up on spiritual wings as eagles, the message of Christ needs to be proclaimed in military chapels.

As long as there are marines who want to storm the beaches with the Lord beside them, the message of Christ needs to be proclaimed in military chapels.

As long as there are sailors who want to anchor their souls on the solid rock, the message of Christ needs to be proclaimed in military chapels.

As long as there are spouses and children who desire to be a part of the family of God, the message of Christ needs to be proclaimed in military chapels.

As a military chaplain, my husband has had countless opportunities to boldly preach the gospel from the pulpit of a military chapel. I am eager to get to heaven and rejoice with the soldiers, sailors, airmen, and marines who received Christ as the result of a chaplain's ministry, gathering together around the throne. My husband considers the chaplaincy's mission to be more important than any other organization. For where other organizations may have significant impact on current or future circumstances, the chaplaincy's mission reaches to eternity. You see:

God didn't send His only Son to save a piece of military hardware.

Jesus didn't die on a cross to protect our freedom of speech.

The Lord didn't come forth from the tomb on Easter morning in support of national interests.

He came to earth because within each of us is a soul that will never die.

Military chaplains come from all faiths and have a unique role in the military. "They are commissioned officers, yet they fill all the roles of religious leaders — spiritual leader, counselor, teacher, and friend." While they are required to reach out to all personnel and their families, serving people of all faiths, they are not asked to compromise their religious convictions. My husband has never been asked to dilute the gospel message. A military chaplain has a clear understanding of the culture in which he is asked to serve.

Have you prayed for a military chaplain lately? Have you spoken words of encouragement to them as they carry out their duty to God and country?

— Brenda

How, then, can they call on the one they have not believed in? And how can they believe in the one of whom they have not heard? And how can they hear without someone preaching to them? And how can they preach unless they are sent? As it is written, "How beautiful are the feet of those who bring good news!"

—Romans 10:14-15

Father, thank You for chaplains who are serving You around the world. May these soldiers of the cross carry Your truth to military personnel and sense Your presence in a powerful way. Encourage them, protect them, guide them, and use them. May Your truth be boldly proclaimed in military chapels, and may they truly be beacons of hope on military installations.

Purple Heart

Given for unusual bravery

resulting in wounds

bravery is a word that speaks of courage in action. And the *Purple Heart* is given when wounds are sustained as part of that action. The military family must possess a courageous spirit in order to endure a lifestyle that requires continuous emotional and physical transition. But character is built and valuable lessons are learned when prayer and commitment accompany these major adjustments in life.

Drippy, Dark Sin

Okay, I know "Drippy, Dark Sin" is a pretty depressing title for a devotional thought. It certainly isn't the most encouraging theme to start or end a day with. But please bear with me. You'll see where I'm going with this.

While my husband was stationed in Yongsan, South Korea, I loved to walk to my destination, wherever I was going. Everything was convenient, and in the summer when the weather was hot and humid, it just made more sense. If I had driven, I would have almost been back home by the time the car had cooled off anyway. So I walked just about everywhere I went—especially on Saturdays. I would put on my walking shoes and go to the PX (Post Exchange), the Shopette (convenience store), or anywhere I wanted to go.

One Saturday, I had been walking for quite some time to pick up a couple of things for the week. I had even stopped to visit a friend and stayed for coffee. Before heading home, though, I decided to see what wonderful new things had come in to the Chosun that I just had to have. The Chosun was a gift store that received shipments from around Asia, where we could purchase all kinds of unique items while living in Korea. It was operated by wives, mostly on a volunteer basis.

I stopped by the outside area and saw a friend of mine. She was standing with the new Commanding General's wife, who had just flown in that week to settle in with her husband for their tour. We talked for a while. I began to feel moisture running down my face and told her that the humidity in Korea had been a big surprise for me. I said something about how I never expected the heat to be as bad as it was in Korea. She was very kind. We said, "Nice to meet you," and I was on my way home.

By the time I got in the door, I was soaked all over with perspiration. (I believe in the South we call it "glowing.") So I fixed a cold glass of tea and went upstairs to change.

As I looked in the mirror, though, I was quite startled. On the white visor I had been wearing, a black, circular stain had formed. And where the sweat had been dripping down my face, I now had dark streaks in its path.

You see, I had thought that instead of paying to have the

gray hair colored around my face, I would just use a rinse to keep it calmed down a bit. I immediately realized, though, what had just happened. As I had been talking with the new commanding general's wife, black sweat had been rolling down my cheeks, and my white hat had been stained in a perfect outline around my face.

I stood there, half laughing and half crying, wondering if the next time I saw her, I could even look her in the eye. I immediately began scrubbing my face, dropped my hat in a sink full of cold water, and poured in some bleach to try to get the stain out before it set. As I watched the stain soak out, and looked to see my face clean and fresh again, it hit me: When I meet my "Commander" in the heavenlies, the last thing I want is for the evidence of black sin to be dripping from my life. How I want to meet Him with a clean face, clean attire, a clean heart, and a clean life, so that He will say to me, "Well done, my good and faithful servant." My heart's desire is to stand before Him unashamed and untarnished by life's circumstances. Oh, how He wants us to continually be on our knees so that He can cleanse us daily—from all the drippy, dark sin that would keep us from His perfect love!

How does the old hymn go?

Whiter than snow, yes, whiter than snow,
Now wash me and I shall be whiter than snow.

—*Carol*

If we confess our sins, he is faithful and just
and will forgive us our sins and purify us
from all unrighteousness.

—1 John 1:9

I came into Your presence, Lord,
With sin all over me;
I quickly looked around,
because I knew all the world could see.

The things that I had done
Were simply in clear view;
All I wanted was to stand pure in front of You.

I asked for Your forgiveness;
My sins were washed away.
I am so thankful, Lord, for You
and give thanks to You each day.
Amen.

Packing Up

When my husband entered the Army, we had already made seven moves on our own. Whether it was a move from one apartment to another across town, or a move across country, we decided quickly it was not among our favorite activities.

So the news that Uncle Sam was going to be sending a work crew to pack us up and move us out was good news to us. This military choice seemed like a good one in my book!

Our packing day arrived, and I was impressed with the crew that came to help us, wearing their neat little jump-suits and working in such a professional manner. I thought to myself how sharp and knowledgeable they were. They were doing me such a grand favor, I could not have thought any less.

Soon thereafter, we reached our first duty station in Fort Benning, Georgia. After several weeks of waiting in the military guest house, we were finally able to sign for a beautiful set of historic quarters at the home of the Army infantry. Life was good!

Imagine my horror, though, when I began unpacking those sleek, perfect boxes, packed by those sharp, profes-sional packers, only to find inside—garbage! They had packed my garbage! One open box held rotten bananas, a moldy milk-encrusted baby bottle, and other examples of disgusting waste and rubbish. Unbelievable!

Looking back on this, I have to smile. I had been so thrilled with the fact that I did not have to pack and move myself, and so impressed with the snappy, well-dressed movers, I had failed to see what was being packed.

These thoughts lead me to ask myself: What garbage do I continue to box up and pack in my inner life?

One often thinks that things will get better with the next move, with the next exciting chapter of life. Too often, however, we just pack up the same problems. Eventually the box must be reopened, and the stench of the rubbish will become apparent again.

If you find yourself in this place, I encourage you to find help. Often we need more than church attendance or Bible study involvement to face the garbage that is packed in our lives. Military chaplains are available for counseling or to direct you to other sources of professional help. There are also Christian ministries that exist for the sole purpose of making a difference in your life when you are unable to help yourself.

Garbage left untreated will continue to follow us until we decide to throw it out for good.

—Brenda

"Forget the former things; do not dwell on the past. See, I am doing a new thing! Now it springs up; do you not perceive it? I am making a way in the desert and streams in the wasteland."

—Isaiah 43:18-19

Dear Lord, too often I encounter thoughts from the past that cause me to lose my joy. Your Word tells me not to dwell on the past but to trust You for a new thing! Give me courage to look at the future with hope, knowing You will make a way—even in the desert places of my life. Amen.

Door to Door

Everyone in the military knows one or two horror stories concerning moves. One of my husband's CGSC (Command and General Staff College) classmates lost all of his things at the bottom of the Pacific Ocean when moving from Guam. Even as I write, I have just heard of a friend who moved from Israel in April and has not heard (as of September) where her family's worldly possessions have located themselves.

The military family always longs for the "perfect move." Our move from Fort Leavenworth, Kansas, to Fort Bragg, North Carolina (we thought) was going to be just that.

By now we had some experience with moving like this, so we believed we had hit upon the perfect plan. My husband would leave the day after the packers and would meet them at the door of our new home. No storage, no waiting—the perfect "door to door" move.

Richard arrived at the house right on time. But the moving van did not. Day one passed. Day two. Day three. At this point, he began to inquire about things. The moving company responded that the truck had encountered some mechanical difficulties. They assured him, though, that our belongings were on their way.

Day four. Day five. Day six. Finally, the moving company contacted Richard and confessed that they indeed had not heard from the moving crew. They did get a call from someone in Virginia, however, who reported that a truck which bore their company name and number had been abandoned on the side of the interstate.

Our perfect move, needless to say, had met with a major detour. We waited anxiously to see what damage might have occurred. Amazingly, our things were fine. They had received only minor water damage from a hole that had resulted when the truck ran off the side of the road.

The Lord continually reminds me that this world—and the things of this world—are temporary. I can relate to the story of Abraham repeated in the book of Hebrews:

By faith Abraham, when called to go to a place
he would later receive as his inheritance, obeyed and
went, even though he did not know where he was going.
By faith he made his home in the promised land like a
stranger in a foreign country; he lived in tents, as did
Isaac and Jacob, who were heirs with him of the same
promise. For he was looking forward to the city with
foundations, whose architect and builder is God.

—Hebrews 11:8-10

What kept Abraham and Sarah going was the final destination. It is what keeps me going as well. There is great liberty in knowing that this world is not my home. My husband and I may one day have that "door to door" move, but there is only one "perfect" move. The move I make from this world to my heavenly home—that will be perfect! *—Brenda*

Oh Lord, I can get so settled and attached to this world. Thank You for reminding me through this military lifestyle that my life on earth is temporary. Help me today to have an eternal perspective. May I rejoice in the fact that I am an heir of the promised inheritance of eternal life with You. Amen.

Attack on the Comfort Zone

I have my favorite places to be comfortable, don't you? Sometimes my living room is a comfort zone, where there is no TV or distraction of any kind. I can be comfortable reading or writing or praying there. It might also be outside under the sun umbrella on the back porch, reading the morning paper with my first cup of coffee. I truly have these familiar "zones" where I am almost complacent as I retreat to do things that do not require much effort.

Even as Christians, we have such a tendency to find and stay in our comfort zones. We sit in the same seat at church.

We go to Bible studies with the same women we see in church. We pray with the same prayer partner who has been with us for years. After years of spilling our problems and difficulties in life with a few close friends, we have a tendency to stay with these people in order to avoid getting "real" with others.

These are not necessarily bad things; they are just points that might cause us to become complacent or lax in our Christian walk.

One of the blessings of military life is that we are continually taken out of our comfort zones. We get to know our neighbors—then we move. We get to know our church—then we move. Our kids meet best friends in school and in the neighborhood—then we move. We develop friendships with people we can share and pray and cry with—then we move.

I once heard it said, "A military wife never gets fired! Her husband just gets orders!" And so, we move. . . .

I believe God gives the military wife supernatural strength to deal with these situations. He takes us from moving to a house to making it a home. Then He takes us from moving to another house to making another home. He shows us how we can meet friends who become sisters, then He moves us on to more friends who increase our sisterhood. We are never able to stay fully attached to any one comfort zone. We are continually growing and stretching and expanding the comfort level to expand our witness and give us boldness for Christ.

The Bible promises, "In all your ways acknowledge him, and he will make your paths straight" (Proverbs 3:6). This is a promise which says I must continue to keep going; otherwise, the Lord would not have told me about the path I was meant to tread. This path is designed for my continual walk, not my stagnation in a comfort zone. It is a path that allows me to serve Him by being open to change, new experiences, and new surroundings.

This is why I can be thankful for the time spent moving, traveling, and making new friends at each stop along the way.

—Carol

"I will give you a new heart and put a new spirit in you; I will remove from you your heart of stone and give you a heart of flesh."
—Ezekiel 36:26

Lord, thank You for never letting me get comfortable in my life. Keep me moving continually forward . . . toward You. Amen.

A Hidden Gem

After about six weeks in Seoul, Korea, we were slowly becoming acquainted with the new and foreign culture. The children had made some friends, and school was in full swing. My husband's job was keeping him challenged and busy. I had even taken that great leap of my own and volunteered for a few activities.

But I still felt lost and lonely. We had left behind a close-knit fellowship of wonderful friends. The Lord had blessed our previous assignment by putting us within a few hours' driving distance from both our families. The disappointment of leaving a situation like that takes time to heal.

Upon coming to a new duty station, there is always the painful task of re-entering. I often think it would be much easier if we could carry around a resumé with us, like someone new to the job market. We could pass it out to our new neighbors, and it would instantly tell them why we would make such a great neighbor and friend. We could take it to all of the organizations we would like to be involved in and, instead of timidly volunteering to do the simplest, most menial tasks, we could instantly prove to others how we had chaired the most successful event ever at our last installation.

It was during one of these lonely times that I was volunteering at a gift shop called the Chosun, run by the Officers Wives Club. As Carol mentioned in an earlier story, the Chosun is a shop that has treasures from all over the Orient. The money generated from the shop provides wonderful services in the community and beyond.

On one particular occasion, I had spent the entire day there—opening, packing, and unpacking boxes, checking merchandise for customers. At some point in the mid-afternoon, I remember lovingly reaching down to touch the beautiful ring my husband had presented me that summer for our wedding anniversary. Feeling something amiss, I jerked my hand up and sadly saw that one of the diamonds was gone!

I began hopelessly retracing my steps, as did everyone

else in the shop. Disappointedly, I resigned myself to the fact that the stone was probably lost forever. I knew in itself it was only a material thing that could be replaced. My disappointment, though, was in the value that something given in such love was damaged and lost.

When I arrived home, I asked my sons to agree with me in prayer that if the stone was anywhere to be found, we could locate it. After praying, I opened my purse and took out my wallet to see if I had enough change to take a taxi to the commissary. As I counted the change—there among the copper pennies, silver dimes, and nickels—a beautiful little diamond sparkled up at me!

That tiny stone could have been anywhere! I had walked to work and back, as well as all over the shop. The boxes I had packed for people were being sent all over the world. I thought how, out of all the possible places this gem could have fallen from its setting, what more perfectly safe place could it have found than my protective, snapped-shut change purse?

My children and I immediately thanked the Lord for the miracle, and I straightaway called the women of the gift shop to tell them the news. As I thought about these events, the Holy Spirit turned on a light of truth for me. I was being challenged to trust Him in this new situation and this new place—Seoul, Korea. Just like that diamond, I felt very much out of place and lost. The Lord spoke so clearly to my heart that in His time, I would be placed in the setting that He had prepared for me. Until then, He knew exactly where I was—safe, protected, and sheltered in His loving hand.

The following verse describes a time when the children of Israel were lost and lonely. The promise given to them is also ours to claim in times of loneliness.

—*Brenda*

The Lord their God will save them on that day as the flock of his people. They will sparkle in his land like jewels in a crown.

—Zechariah 9:16

My heavenly Father, Your thoughts toward me are amazing! You show me in such tangible ways how great Your love is for me. Thank You for bringing me to this place, at this time. I know that it is Your plan, even though I may not feel settled or at home. This assignment was ordained for me, and I look forward to seeing how You will use me to build Your Kingdom in this place. May I shine for You, confident that You are in control of my life. Amen.

Up in Smoke

*O*nce while we were living in Korea, my sister-in-law, Diane, made plans to come visit us. We were looking forward to a trip to Hong Kong, and much shopping was on the agenda. I had made my lists and checked them twice.

During my quiet time the morning prior to Diane's visit, however, I was reading in 1 John 2 from *The Message*:

> Don't love the world's ways. Don't love the world's goods. Love of the world squeezes out love for the Father. Practically everything that goes on in the world—wanting your own way, wanting everything for yourself, wanting to appear important—has nothing to do with the Father. It just isolates you from him. The world and all its wanting, wanting, wanting is on the way out—but whoever does what God wants is set for eternity.
>
> —1 John 2:15-17

I had to chuckle as I looked from the words in my Bible to the words on my "wish list." So I prayed that morning, asking the Lord to help me with my desire to accumulate things. I purposely rededicated all of my possessions to Him for His use.

Later in the morning, I needed to run an errand. And as I opened my apartment door upon my return, I was met with a cloud of billowing smoke. I rushed to my neighbor's house to call the fire department.

As the firemen were in my apartment, extinguishing whatever was causing the smoke, I stood in the parking lot, looking up. A friend came over and asked if I was okay. I said, yes, I was fine. In fact, I was better than fine! I told her "I gave everything to the Lord this morning, and He took it! It's all gone up in smoke! And I'm okay with it!"

As I stood there, I thought of all the things I had not lost: my husband, my children, my family and friends, my health, my relationship with my Lord. I felt blessed! Really!

Soon, a fireman came out with what appeared to be a charred disk. I had been so preoccupied with my plans for the trip, I had placed a package of frozen tortillas in the microwave, and had punched in fifteen minutes instead of five for them to thaw. Everything had not gone up in smoke, although things were a little smoky for awhile. The microwave never recovered, but it was a small loss compared to what it could have been.

Diane and I had a wonderful, memory-making trip to Hong Kong. I approached our shopping, however, with a different perspective. I did bring home treasures that I still take great delight in, but they are primarily a visible reminder of God's blessings to me.

Military families have opportunities to see the world and enjoy homes filled with lovely reminders of travel and adventure. It is very easy to get attached to my things and hold on tightly to them. The Word of God, though, tells us that someday the things of this world really will go up in smoke! Until then I must hold earthly possessions with a loose hand, never allowing my "wanting" to isolate me from my Father in heaven.

—Brenda

Father, today I dedicate my possessions to You. Whether they are great or small, they are only things; and as such, they will someday fade away. Help me to lay up treasure in heaven today that will not be exhausted, where no thief comes near and no moth destroys. For where my treasure is, there my heart will be also (Luke 12:33-34). Amen.

Pray for Your Children

Prayer is such a gift from God to us. He has given us the privilege of communicating with Him. He doesn't need this communication to be God. He doesn't need our concerns brought before Him, because He knows exactly what those concerns are. He doesn't need to hear our requests for the president's protection or the healing of our parents. He just wants it! He desires it! This communication is very important to Him. It teaches us how to get to know Him by depending on Him to help us and comfort us.

I truly began understanding prayer from a very early age. I had praying parents, as well as praying grandparents and a praying extended family. For as long as I can remember, I was blessed to be around people who thanked God and asked for His guidance.

That said, I feel as though I really began my own prayer

journey sometime in my late thirties to early forties. It was a journey initiated by my becoming a mother, wanting to cover my children with prayer and to know that God was going before them and behind them, protecting them with His guardian angels.

I had a dear friend ask me once if I prayed for my children. Being somewhat offended, I said, "Well, of course I do!" She said, "Do you pray out loud for them?" I told her, "No"—that I mostly prayed for them while they were away, or during my quiet times, or whenever the Lord brought them to my mind. She began sharing with me, though, the importance of praying out loud for my children. She said they need to hear the prayers of a mother's heart, because it teaches them how to pray for others.

When our older son was twelve and our younger son was ten, I told them that each morning before they left the house, we would hold hands at the door, and I was going to begin to pray out loud for them before they left for the day. They were fine with that. Being the ages they were, it wasn't hard to get them to do what their mother said. So each morning, they would gather their backpacks and coats and come to the front door, where we would hold hands and I would pray.

My prayer would go something like this: "Lord, thank You for this day. Thank You that You have given another day for my boys to enjoy and share with their friends and schoolmates. I pray that on this day You will let them find favor with their teachers and that they will be covered with the blood of Jesus as they go about their activities. I pray, Lord, for a hedge of protection to be around them that will prick the enemy if he comes near them. Lord, thank You for our sons and for what they mean to us as parents. And thank You for Your love for them. In Jesus' name. Amen."

If there was a test or a report due on that day, we would pray for specifics. They would then trot out the door. They knew that no one was leaving until we prayed.

As the years went on into high school, friends would come by in the mornings to catch a ride to school. We would invite them in and ask if they had prayer requests. Then we would pray for them.

I will never forget one morning in particular, when the boys were in junior high. We were stationed at Fort Leavenworth, Kansas, and our older son had terrible allergies. Because we had not had time after school the day before to get his allergy shot, we were having to go early that morning to do it. Finding ourselves in a rush, I prayed for our younger son, sent him out the door, then left in the car with our older son for the clinic. We arrived there, got his shot, waited the fifteen minutes to ensure there was no reaction, and then headed off to school. I ran in, he took off to his class, I signed him in and left.

That afternoon, I was baking breadsticks as they came in the door from school. Our older son stomped into the kitchen and flung his backpack across the floor.

"Mom," he said, "You didn't pray for me this morning, did you?"

I said, "Well, now that you mention it, I guess we did get in an awful hurry. Why?"

"Today, I was at the drinking fountain just getting a drink," he said, "and these three big guys were walking down the hall towards me. When they got to me, they just pushed me down on the hard floor. It really hurt. I looked up at them and I said [as he was pointing at them from the floor] 'MY MOM DID NOT PRAY FOR ME TODAY!'"

What joy filled my heart—not that he had been bullied, of course—but that he had put the connection together between prayer and real life. He realized that when we don't pray, we open ourselves up for attack.

Precious mother, they are listening and they are watching. Never give up. Never cease in your prayers.

—*Carol*

*Devote yourselves to prayer,
being watchful and thankful.*
—Colossians 4:2

Father, do not ever let me become complacent or discouraged while lifting my children in prayer. Whether they be under our roof or away on their own, I want to be at Your throne on their behalf. Amen.

A Porcelain Box and Trouser Socks

Our family had just moved to Fort Bragg, North Carolina, where my husband had been assigned as a chaplain for the 82nd Airborne. This was an assignment he had longed for, and I was trying to be happy for him. For various reasons, though, I did not want to be in North Carolina. I was still adjusting to the idea.

Okay, truth be known, I was not adjusting to the idea at all. In fact, I was in outright rebellion!

This became really clear to me one unhappy morning, while I begrudgingly prepared to make the thirty-minute trek to Fort Bragg to attend Bible study. As I rushed out the door, I became aware of the trouser socks I had put on, which were gradually sliding down my ankle and around my heel. I pulled them up in disgust and headed out of the house, knowing I would already be late for the opening session of the meeting.

I arrived at the building where the gathering was held—still feeling rushed, restless, and frustrated. Just walking to the entrance took more time than it should, as I continually had to reach down to pull up my socks. I went inside and sat down beside my friend, who took one look at me and asked, "What is wrong with you?" I responded that I could not find this, did something with that, had to drive behind a convoy, and besides all of that—I was about to lose my religion over my trouser socks!

Needless to say, I did not get much out of the Bible study. In fact, I remember leaving early and driving home, fussing at God and wondering if He had any clue where I was and what I was doing.

As I pulled into my driveway, I noticed a package sitting on the doorstep. It was from a very good friend, who for months had been telling me she was preparing a surprise to send me. I had all but forgotten about this until I noticed her return address. So as I plopped myself into my kitchen floor (after removing my socks, of course!), I began opening the package.

My eyes filled with tears as I opened treasure after treasure from the heart of my friend. Each gift was wrapped beautifully. It was as if someone had gone into a store and began pulling things off the shelf, knowing that each one was something I would love!

I came to what I thought was the last box. Carefully opening it, I caught my breath as I took out a lovely Limóges porcelain heart box. I began to weep as I thought of how unworthy I was to receive such an outpouring of love. God had used this friend and her generosity to shower upon me lovely things when I had been so ugly and bitter.

I thought I had depleted the contents of the box, but as I looked under all the packing peanuts, my hand touched another package. This one was not wrapped beautifully. In fact, it was quite tacky! It was ripped and mangled and had sale prices stamped all over it. It looked as if it had been a last-minute toss into the box.

I laughed and cried as I realized that I was holding in my hand a package of . . . trouser socks!

—*Brenda*

You know when I sit and when I rise; you perceive my thoughts from afar. You discern my going out and my lying down; you are familiar with all my ways. Before a word is on my tongue you know it completely, O Lord. You hem me in——behind and before; you have laid your hand upon me. Such knowledge is too wonderful for me, too lofty for me to attain.

—Psalm 139:2-6

Dear Father, You are so loving and faithful to Your children. It is hard for me to imagine that You care so personally for me, and yet I know it is true. You involve Yourself in my life! Help me today to be involved in the lives of others. Show me ways to reach out to those who may be lonely, frustrated, and needy. May I reach out to others as You have reached out to me. Amen.

Section Three
Bronze Star

Given for heroic or meritorious achievement

Military wives have been described as heroes on the home front. This is an apt description of the women who support their warrior husbands. They are often called upon to accept added responsibility during their husbands' military career, as many redeployed husbands will confirm. The wise woman will draw on the resources of family, friends, and faith to cope during these times.

My Father's Hand

Unaccompanied assignments are something a military family must often face. For some, the orders that hold this news are a reason to leave the military. For others, it is an opportunity for a great adventure. I have even known some military wives who actually traveled on their own to a destination where their husbands were asked to serve unaccompanied. Most of the time this means no installation housing, as well as the many other challenges of a non-command sponsored assignment.

The majority of military wives, however, fall into another category. These are the women who stay behind and wait. I am always amazed by the courage it takes to do this. How do you choose which year to miss from the life of your child?

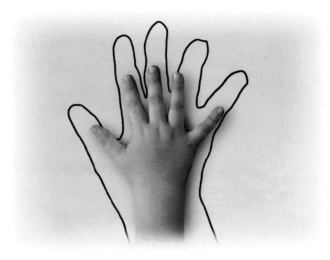

What can you do to make Dad still active and remain Dad?

One creative friend came up with a beautiful idea. Dad drew a picture of his hand and left it for his child. Any time the child felt lonely and longed for the touch of his father's hand, all he had to do was place his hand in the outline of that picture.

It sounds like such a simple act, but my friend reported that the results were amazing! Through this picture came the understanding that Daddy was thinking of him, praying for him, and loving him. This picture of his daddy's hand gave him great comfort when time and distance kept them separated.

Sometimes it seems as if God has taken a remote, unaccompanied assignment and is far away from us. The distance seems too great to span. Our prayers seem unable to reach His ear. The insecurity of this temporal life can often engulf our thoughts and actions. These are the times when we must look for His handprints in our lives and in our world: the laugh of a little child; blue skies; mountains; the love of family and friends.

God's Word tells us that there is nothing that can snatch us out of His hand. You can rest secure in the knowledge that He is holding you tight!

—Brenda

"I give them eternal life, and they shall never perish; no one can snatch them out of my hand. My Father, who has given them to me, is greater than all; no one can snatch them out of my Father's hand. I and the Father are one."

—John 10:28-30

Father of grace and mercy, I place myself in Your hands today. Remind me in those moments of insecurity that You are holding me tight. Let the peace and confidence of this knowledge envelop me, and may I be an agent of Your peace to others. Amen.

When It All Comes Crashing Down

During Richard's first assignment at Fort Benning, Georgia, he was tasked to go on a month-long military exercise in Germany called REFORGER. I was not eager for this separation, but I worked diligently at being as prepared as possible.

We endeavored to get all our ducks in a row before I was left at home for a whole month as a single parent with two preschoolers:

- Cars serviced (Richard even bought a new one so it would be sure to be reliable!) — CHECK
- Power of attorney — CHECK
- Financial information — CHECK

We were ready!

Looking back, the anxiety I felt seems rather silly in light of the lengthy separations others have endured. It was our first one, however, so it was high drama for us!

The boys and I did very well while Richard was away. I planned many activities to keep them busy and occupied. Richard sent them cards and other treats as regularly as he could. (This was in the days before e-mail. How quickly times have changed!)

I had heard from others, tongue-in-cheek, that if anything was going to go wrong, it would happen while my husband was deployed. True to form, then—midway through this separation—Fort Benning was hit with a major ice storm, which was very unusual for a town in the deep South!

I was awakened in the middle of the night to the sound of water dripping in an area of the house where water was not supposed to drip. I walked into the living room to find water pouring down the walls. I ran to my neighbor's house and pleaded for help.

Several neighbors came to help me move my furniture. (Of course, the living room was the only room in the house that had new furniture!) The cold weather had frozen the pipes in the house, and the radiator pipes in the upstairs had frozen and burst. To make matters worse, there were so many other, greater emergencies on the installation because of the weather, our work order was low on the priority list. As a result, what began as a leak down the walls ended up being a ceiling completely caved in!

Does it ever feel like everything is crashing down around you? Sometimes, even when the boxes are all checked and you have prepared yourself fully and faithfully, the unexpected storm comes and the ceiling caves in. Life happens. We live in a sinful world where we are too often surprised by events and circumstances that result in damage.

When my living room ceiling caved in, all I knew to do was cry for help! So when circumstances get out of control and it feels like the walls are crashing in around you:

1. *Cry out to the Lord for help.* He desires to help us out of our trouble.

"Then they cried out to the Lord in their trouble, and he brought them out of their distress. He stilled the storm to a whisper; the waves of the sea were hushed. They were glad when it grew calm, and he guided them to their desired haven" (Psalm 107:28-30).

2. *Cry out to others for help.* When you are struggling with difficult circumstances, be willing to be vulnerable with others and allow them to comfort and help you.

"Carry each other's burdens, and in this way you will fulfill the law of Christ" (Galatians 6:2).

—Brenda

 *God of all help, there are times when it feels like the world is crashing down around me. Sometimes I do not hold up well and I feel timid to ask for help. I cry out to You today to still the storms in my life. Help me be willing to be vulnerable and ask for the help of others. You have placed people around me who will help me if I just ask. Give me opportunities today to carry someone's burden and fulfill Your law of love. Amen.*

Hurry Up and Wait

For months the rumor mill had been saying that deployment for my husband was going to be a reality. But I pushed the thoughts of his having to leave to the back of my mind. Surely they would not need him to go to Afghanistan.

The word came in April, though, that deployment was definitely a possibility. And by May the possibility was looking more and more inevitable. The word on the street in June was that they would be leaving in September. But by the time July rolled around, the message came that they would more than likely be gone by the first of the year.

One Saturday afternoon in August, however, as my husband was preparing to fly to Atlanta, the call came for him to get to headquarters and begin packing up to leave for Afghanistan. . . on Tuesday! So our lives moved quickly into high gear, trying to think of all the things we needed to do in three days to be ready for him to be gone for what could be a full year!

Fortunately, we had completed the checklist of deployment necessities in anticipation of what would come. He had come home with published lists of what to pack in each bag. It was quite an impressive exhibit of military ingenuity. Every detail had been thought out with great precision. Seeing this display of meticulous planning actually gave me great confidence. A military that plans this precisely in packing a rucksack, I figured, would certainly take every precaution to protect my husband in enemy territory.

So by Monday he was packed and ready to ship out.

Tuesday came, though, and Richard remained.

Wednesday came, and Richard remained.

Thursday came, and Richard remained.

Friday came, and still . . . Richard remained. At this point the frantic call he had received the week before to hurry up and get ready seemed absurd.

An entry from my journal during that week reads: "I find myself feeling in limbo. Part of me wants Richard to go ahead and go so life can become whatever 'normal' is going to be. Then I feel guilty in case something was to happen to him. I don't want him to go, yet I feel eager to rise to the occasion. He seems to have great peace. I fluctuate between peace and fear. The reality that he is going to a very dangerous location is ever present in my mind. I will pray specifically for 1) God's perfect timing in his departure, and 2) Good use of the time we have together."

We finally decided that we had a choice: we could be frustrated at having to wait, or we could make the best use of the time and enjoy ourselves. I am so glad we chose the latter. The last few days of our time together at home were fun and pleasant memories for us both.

As Christians we are told to "watch and wait" for Christ's return. Just as my husband finally received a call to take those packed bags and load them on a military plane, we will be called to join Christ in heaven. Whether it is through death or His second coming, we are to be prepared.

But we have a choice as to how we will wait. Although I often get homesick for heaven, I also am aware that there is a purpose for me here on earth. Until the time that the final call comes, I want to be actively involved in helping others prepare for the call.

—*Brenda*

"Therefore keep watch, because you do not know on what day your Lord will come. . . . So you also must be ready, because the Son of Man will come at an hour when you do not expect him."
—Matthew 24:42, 44

Oh God, I am homesick for Heaven.
This imperfect body will be perfect;
These impure thoughts will be pure;
The tension of flesh and spirit will be no more;
The frustration of comparing what could be
*   to what is will not arise.*
Perfect, pure, peaceful,
Fulfilled potential in Your presence. Amen.

D - Day

Journal entry — August 23, 2002

Deployment Day finally arrived. I am experiencing a myriad of emotions: sadness, fear, excitement. The excitement is not the happy type of anticipatory excitement, but more of getting ready to travel into unknown territory. I want to do a good job at this. Everyone seems so concerned for how I am going to handle Richard being away. I am so ready to figure out what this is going to look like. On the one hand, the temporary nature of it makes aspects of Richard's absence seem attractive. However, when I speak of anything positive or remotely good on my part, I am stuck with guilt. I quietly push any good aside. Isn't this an interesting way to approach deployment? Should I force myself to look at the good, or is it just that I feel a need to wait until he is gone? I find myself suppressing thoughts and feelings.

Journal entry—August 27, 2002

Richard left a week ago today. One week down, how many more to go? I'm feeling somewhat overwhelmed by all the things I need to do. There are quirks in an insurance payment, a phone bill, and our moving claim. It is uncanny that these unusual things happen right after he leaves; they say, however, that this is the way it always is. The temptation is to turn on the tube, push the remote, and put it all off. I don't want to do that, though. I want to deal with this and conquer! Lord, help me to get things accomplished that I have been putting off. Make my hands productive and my mind sharp. Be my counselor, husband, motivator, encourager, sustainer, and friend.

Deployment is something that is very real for military families. For those of us who are left behind, it can be a time of loneliness and stress.

At the time of this writing, my husband has been deployed to Afghanistan for almost five months. For the most part I have been fine. I have stayed busy doing volunteer work, visiting family and friends, and writing. I encounter some surprise moments, however, when waves of loneliness engulf me. The weekend is the worst time for this. I have come to expect it now, and so I prepare myself for the surprise "attack" of emotion.

Saturday mornings, Richard and I enjoy going to a favorite coffee shop for breakfast. Going alone just isn't the same. Sunday comes and—more weeks than not—I have found myself weeping on the way home from chapel. Something about coming home alone for Sunday dinner has been difficult. One week a friend called and asked me to come to her chapel for the Sunday potluck. I had made some other plans, but receiving the invitation took the edge off the morning.

Do you know someone who has a husband deployed? Here are some things you can do to encourage her this week:

· Invite her to lunch after church or chapel on Sunday.

· E-mail her on the weekend. One special friend e-mails me a prayer during the weekends Richard has been away.

· Ask your husband if he would be willing to do any heavy work that your friend could not do alone. After a storm a coworker of Richard's called to see if there was any tree damage that needed to be taken care of.

· Surprise her with a small gift left on her doorstep. I love the comforting taste and smell of vanilla. Last week I found a "comfort" basket on my doorstep filled with vanilla goodies!

· Send a card of encouragement. It has been so encouraging to know that people are praying for both Richard and me.

The Lord has been faithful to our family during this time. I have appreciated my friends and family more than ever. While it is not something I would choose, it has been an experience I will cherish.

—Brenda

Religion that God our Father accepts
as pure and faultless is this: to look after
orphans and widows in their distress.

—James 1:27

Father, please protect our soldiers, airmen, sailors, and marines who are deployed to distant lands. Provide travel mercies, safety from enemy attacks, wisdom in dealing with decisions, and personal health. Put Your supernatural shield of protection about them. Be their helper and their daily strength and encouragement. Use this time to bring families that are separated closer together and closer to You. Make me more aware of those who are experiencing deployment. Give me creative and thoughtful ways to reach out to them and be Your hand extended during this time of separation. Amen.

Timing

I have always believed that the Lord has worked through the military system to take us right where He wanted us to be, right at the time He wanted us to be there. It has often taken me more time than I would have liked in order to get to that place, but it has always proved to be so.

That is, I have always thought this until now.

At the time of this writing, my husband has just returned from a deployment to Afghanistan. We both rejoiced at the news that he would be returning home after six months. We eagerly planned how we would spend the last few months of this assignment before our next move in July.

Richard arrived home on a Saturday, and on Monday the call came that his unit had received yet another deployment order. This time he would leave for an undisclosed area close to Iraq. We were both stunned. I felt disappointed and sad. I also felt afraid.

As I write this, my husband is packing his bags. The scenario we went through just a few months ago is being repeated. It seems strange and surreal. I cannot help but question God's timing.

I received a message from a friend today, asking me to pray for a young twenty-one year-old woman who was just married. Her young husband has also received deployment orders, and she is feeling fear. I can only imagine that she, too, is questioning God's timing as her young husband is called to a faraway land. Perhaps some of you who are reading this are experiencing these same emotions of disappointment, sadness, and fear.

When Richard left for Afghanistan, I felt for the most part a deep sense of peace in God's timing. I trusted that He would protect my husband and bring him safely home. Why, then, am I struggling with trust for the timing of this new situation? I may never be able to answer that question. You see, for some things there is no good time. Faith says, however, that even if it is not a good time, it can still be God's time.

I read in God's Word that it wasn't a good time for Daniel to be carried into captivity, but it was God's time.

It wasn't a good time for Joseph to be sold into slavery, but it was God's time.

If you had asked Mary and Martha, they would have said it wasn't a good time for Lazarus to die, but it was God's time.

For me, this is not a good time for my husband to redeploy. But as His child, I have to believe it is God's time.

These days I am spending time reminding myself of all the moments in the past when God has proven Himself faithful in my life. The biblical principle of recall is increasing my trust as I prepare to say "farewell" once again to my soldier. As I recognize God's timing in the life of our family thus far,

I can only be encouraged to trust that He has this situation in His hands as well.

—*Brenda*

But I trust in you, O Lord; I say, "You are my God." My times are in your hands; deliver me from my enemies and from those who pursue me. Let your face shine on your servant; save me in your unfailing love.
—Psalm 31:14-16

Dear Lord, when I look with earthly eyes at the situation this world is in, I often become fearful. Remind me in these uncertain times of Your faithfulness to me through the years. Prepare my heart for what is to come. Help me to face the future with the light of Your love shining on my face. May I confidently proclaim that You are my God. Help me to trust You even when I do not understand Your timing. Amen.

Fear Factor

I am your basic "scaredy cat." As a child, I was afraid of thunderstorms, tornadoes, the first day of school, animals, getting lost, swimming pools, lakes, rivers, strangers, the second coming, Russia, driving over bridges or through tunnels—the list could go on and on. My adult fears have taken on a more subtle expression: approval, rejection, acceptance, security.

Having this high "fear factor" quotient, it was a surprise to me that when my husband left for Afghanistan, the number one emotion I experienced was not fear. Instead, I felt a great sense of gratitude to God for His peace. If I was honest, I would probably even have to say I felt some pride in the fact that fear was not one of the emotions I was dealing with. I thought, "How spiritually mature I must be!"

The news that Richard was going to be redeployed to Iraq one month after his return from Afghanistan, however, brought with it the fear that had failed to be present at the first separation. Words from my journal the day after Richard left reveal the pain of these emotions:

"I have not felt able to sit and be still with pen and paper and the Word. I feel the effects of my lack of commitment. Despair is at the door. I feel safest and most comfortable in my bed. I don't want to go outside. Keep the doors and windows closed. I won't have to talk, smile, or dress."

"Richard left yesterday morning. I haven't heard from him. I'm praying this means he arrived safely to the 'mysterious destination.' I feel a lump in my throat and sadness in my spirit. I don't want to do anything or go anywhere. I feel terribly lonely, sad, and afraid."

That morning I made myself sit and open my Bible. The devotion for the day was based on Psalm 27. I was especially struck by the timeliness of verses 1-3 and 13-14:

The Lord is my light and my salvation; Whom shall I fear? The Lord is the defense of my life; Whom shall I dread? When evildoers came upon me to devour my flesh, my adversaries and my enemies, they stumbled and fell. Though a host encamp against me, my heart will not fear; Though war rise against me, in spite of this I shall be confident. . . . I would have despaired unless I had believed that I would see the goodness of the Lord in the land of the living; Wait for the Lord; Be strong, and let your heart take courage; Yes, wait for the Lord.

—Psalm 27:1-3, 13-14 (NASB)

In that time of personal weakness, I was thankful for God's living Word. In that moment of fear He spoke peace, comfort, and courage to my heart. There was no way I could doubt that He knew my situation.

If you are experiencing fear right now, do as I did that day. Go to God's Word and apply it to your situation:

· Write out the things that you fear. After reading this Psalm, I wrote out the things that I feared: war, terrorists, disease, and my husband not returning.

· Write out the things that you dread. The things I dreaded during this time of separation were: being alone, being with people, dealing with issues that Richard usually handled, deciding what to have for dinner, and even going to the gym.

· Ask the Lord to "teach [you] His ways and lead [you] in a level path" (vs. 11). I pondered what would make this time "level" or balanced for me, and concluded it would be consistency, commitment, and courage.

Sisters, there are "fear factors" built into each day, whether it concerns something as drastic as war or as common as walking out your front door. The good news is: the Lord promises that He will be our light and our salvation, and we need not fear. The *NIV Study Bible* states that light was often used in Scripture to symbolize well-being. Do you have that spiritual sense of well-being today? I encourage you to give Him the things you dread and fear. Trust Him to lead you in level paths this day . . . and every day.

—*Brenda*

Dear Father of light and life, today I bring to You the issues in my life that bring me dread and fear. Your Word says that with You I have nothing to fear and nothing to dread. The world situation is one that causes many to look to the future with fear. I know that in Your sovereign plan, however, You are in control. I choose to look to the future with hope and confidence, knowing

I will see "good-
ness in the land of
the living." May
my words bring
hope to someone
who is fearful
today. In Jesus'
name. Amen.

Back to the Desert

The long-awaited reunion with my husband after nine months of deployment for Iraqi Freedom had finally arrived. He called and said that his flight would be well past midnight and I need not come to greet him.

I did not like this plan. I had already bought my flag to wave, and I wanted to be present with the crowd of tired but cheering people. Watching the plane land, hearing the band play, and running to greet Richard held a sense of closure for me. In the end I joined the welcoming throng, and Richard admitted he was glad for the small but meaningful fanfare.

During the days that followed, there were other things that Richard and I did not have the same ideas about. For example, I wanted to hear all the deep thoughts and emotions that being in a war would bring. He, on the other hand, had a very matter-of-fact view of what he had just experienced. While there had been meaningful moments for him, in one sense he was just doing his job. And now that he was home, he had even more jobs to do. Among them were some of the questions he had about decisions I had made with the house and the children while he was away. I felt defensive and insecure with this inquiry. There were times when we both felt frustrated and joked: Didn't he want to go back to the desert? Both of us were struggling with some of our expectations concerning his return home.

Chaplain Glen Bloomstrom, former director of the Army's family life ministry, says the bottom line for successful deployments is "realistic communication about expectations." Communication during this time is critical. When it comes time for reunion, expect adjustments. There will be the obvious role adjustments, but there are other issues to consider, as well.

Surprises normally are not good, especially if they conflict with your husband's expectations. For instance, if he has expected you to save the extra "deployment" money, but you have bought a whole new living room suite with it, there may be a problem! Keep him informed not only about financial issues but also the children's grades, the status of the car, medical issues, and any plans you have made for the future. He does not need to return home expecting one thing and finding something else.

When there is a conflict of expectation, the bottom line is: who has the best way? In a marriage relationship it is a matter of give-and-take and understanding. When it comes to serving the Lord, however, it is a matter of submitting to Him and obeying.

The children of Israel faced this same dilemma as the Lord brought them to the edge of the Promised Land. They thought it was best to go back to Egypt, but the Lord knew it was good to go on. Because they were unwilling to learn what was best, they spent forty years wandering in the desert.

As married couples when we get back together after a deployment or separation, it is a matter of working things out. But when it comes to our relationship with the Lord, we must realize that He is perfect and knows what is best. Even when we do not think it is best, we must submit to His will. And if we are too stubborn, we may be sent back to the desert to learn obedience.

Neither my husband nor I really wanted him to return to the desert, and neither does the Lord really want to send us back. He desires instead to communicate with us, and the expectations He has for us are clearly written in His Word.

—*Brenda*

Because of your great compassion you did not abandon them in the desert. By day the pillar of cloud did not cease to guide them on their path, nor the pillar of fire by night to shine on the way they were to take. You gave your good Spirit to instruct them. You did not withhold your manna from their mouths, and you gave them water for their thirst. For forty years you sustained them in the desert; they lacked nothing, their clothes did not wear out nor did their feet become swollen.

—Nehemiah 9:19-21

Father, I thank You for the desert experiences of life that make me long for Your living water. I thank You for the communication of Your Spirit with me as we have made this journey. I long to be changed as a result of the paths You guide me through. I pray for clear communication with my husband so that our expectations will be realistic and our relationship strong. Thank You for providing us with Your Word, which plainly states Your expectations for my life. Help me to fulfill those expectations today and to live this day with purpose and joy! Amen.

Life in 3D

$\mathcal{I}$ have learned that there will be dark times in this life. I often call these times "living in 3D." They are times when all you feel is depression, dread, and discouragement. It is as if you are wearing those crazy 3D glasses, where everything jumps out to get you and reality is distorted.

The prophet Jeremiah wrote these words from Lamentations 3:2-9 during a 3D time of life. The circumstances of this Old Testament prophet found him lonely and secluded:

"He has driven me away and made me walk in darkness rather than light; indeed, he has turned his hand against me again and again, all day long. He has made my skin and my flesh grow old and has broken my bones. He has besieged me and surrounded me with bitterness and hardship. He has made me dwell in darkness like those long dead. He has walled me in so I cannot escape; he has weighed me down with chains."

Can you not feel the heaviness of the prophet in these words? Have you ever felt like this? Have you ever asked questions like, "Where are You in this, Lord?" Thoughts like these seem to be automatic during times of illness, depression, or transition.

It was in such a time of transition that I was living my life in 3D. I wrote my own lamentation in my journal on August 16, 1996:

"I feel alone. This house is no companion. Television gets old, the boys are uncommunicative, and Richard is too tired when he finally gets home. There's nothing I want to do. Everything seems too hard, too much effort.

"Why did we have to move here? I'm trying to have the right attitude, I'm trying to be positive: 'I think we'll like it.' 'I feel anticipation.' 'It's a good place for the boys.' 'The chapel is great.'—blah, blah, blah.

"Honestly, for today: I don't like it—it's too far away—the town is too small—the house too isolated—the school too big—the carpet dirty—the linoleum scratched—the bathrooms small—the yard scruffy—the carport ugly—the people snooty—the kids grungy—I don't want to be here! Why did you make us come here, Lord? Why?"

During my times of 3D living, I have challenged myself to practice the three Rs. No, this is not the old-fashioned reading, 'riting and 'rithmetic. Instead, it is something we can see modeled by Brother Jeremiah as we continue to read Lamentations 3. He moans his complaints to the Lord (He can take it!), but then he says something key and essential in Lamentations 3:19-21:

"I remember my affliction and my wandering, the bitterness and the gall. I well remember them, and my soul is downcast within me. Yet this I call to mind . . ."

Jeremiah reflects, recalls, and remembers. Reflection is something used throughout the Bible during times of 3D living. As we reflect, recall, and remember God's faithfulness in the past, we can be assured of His faithfulness in the present and the future. Suddenly, the out-of-focus, exaggerated view of life takes on perspective.

Recently, I was asked to share my personal experiences as a military spouse with several young women who are contemplating marriage to a military man. It has brought great satisfaction to reflect, recall, and remember—and then to share with them how wonderful this life can be. I've been careful not to paint too rosy of a picture. But honestly— contrary to the negative press the military too frequently receives—it can be a wonderful lifestyle.

The results of practicing the three Rs can be the same for us as they were for Jeremiah.

—*Brenda*

And therefore I have hope: Because of the Lord's great love we are not consumed, for his compassions never fail. They are new every morning; great is your faithfulness. I say to myself, 'The Lord is my portion; therefore I will wait for him.' The Lord is good to those whose hope is in him, to the one who seeks him; it is good to wait quietly for the salvation of the Lord.

—Lamentations 3:21-26

Father, as I reflect on Your goodness to me, I can recall those times when You have been faithful. I remember the times You comforted and encouraged me. I recall the blessings of life that I enjoy. I remember the wonderful people You have placed in my life through the years, and I am grateful. Today I choose to have hope as I remember Your faithfulness in my life. I will seek You and wait on You to work Your completed will in my life and my circumstances. Amen.

Section Four

Distinguished Service Award

Given for exceptionally meritorious service

The rewards of exceptional service upon retirement are great. Life applications, leadership training, appreciation for traditions, as well as patriotism—all of these and more are instilled within us. There is hope for the future following a job well done.

Boots over the Wire

One day while driving through our military installation, I happened to look up at a telephone wire hung from one side of the street to the other. Draped over the wires were a pair of combat boots tied together by their laces.

I remember thinking how strange this was. I assumed that some soldier in a drunken binge had tied his boots together and thrown them up in the air. Little did I know, however, what significance these ceremoniously placed boots had in military culture.

I soon began noticing that there were other boots thrown across electrical and telephone wires. When I pointed them out to my husband, he responded, "Yeah, someone said goodbye to the military." Apparently, throwing your boots over the wire is symbolic of never having to put them on again. Sometimes the boots were painted a bright color, carrying the message that this was one soldier who was happy to be rid of those boots. I've never seen or heard of anyone climbing up the pole to retrieve their boots. The message is loud and clear: "Good-bye and good riddance!"

Several weeks ago I heard a reporter from a base camp in Saudi Arabia describe "boot hill." When military personnel leave their assignment, they actually have a retirement ceremony for their desert combat boots. There are countless numbers of boots standing in memory of the time spent in this desert outpost, the owners planning never to return.

There are mornings when I rise and recognize the need to throw some boots over a wire. The Lord challenges me to throw the boots of selfishness over the wire. He asks me to throw the boots of wrong motivation over the wire. The list could go on and on.

Too often, though, my problem is: instead of throwing the boots over the wire and ridding myself of the sin in my life, I simply set the boots on the back porch. But it is too easy to retrieve my boots from there and put them back on again. I must be willing to hang them high on the cross of Christ where I cannot climb up and retrieve them.

I can only do this when I make the firm decision that I will not walk down that path again. The choice to walk in righteousness is mine. I have the promise that the Holy Spirit will help me in these decisions.

Today, I choose to fling those boots high and say good-bye to anything that would keep me from walking in the truth of God's Word.

—Brenda

You used to walk in these ways, in the life you once lived. But now you must rid yourselves of all such things as these: anger, rage, malice, slander, and filthy language from your lips. Do not lie to each other, since you have taken off your old self with its practices and have put on the new self, which is being renewed in knowledge in the image of its Creator.

—Colossians 3:7-10

Father, thank You for sending the Holy Spirit to comfort and instruct me in Your ways. His work of conviction is often painful as I see the sin in my life. I pray that anything that is displeasing to You would be revealed to me. I pray that I would walk in the light of Your truth today. Amen.

Support and Exhort

Through the years, I have had many wise, mature, godly women to mentor me. I remember watching as they continually supported and exhorted their husbands and children in ways so unique to the military.

I saw love on their faces as their soldier husbands marched by on the parade field. I saw them in the front row viewing stands, throwing winks and smiles as the change of command and the passing of the colors took place.

I saw their great pride on display when we attended formals where every rank and military branch was represented in full dress uniform. I saw comfort shown by a mother when Dad had to miss yet another special event, ball game, or school program. You might hear them say, "Your dad is serving a country that you will come to love as you grow older, and then you will understand why he is not here."

I saw undeniable closeness felt by families who were separated by short tours, deployment, or TDY (Temporary Duty)—when your best friend truly is your brother, your sister, or your mom or dad . . . to replace the family you are so far away from.

I learned from these women of faith, and from this came such a sense of pride for my own husband. I always brushed away a tear as Richard was presented with special awards and honors for his continued service as the years went by. I gained a sense of knowing that everything he was doing was touching someone somewhere in our country . . . even throughout the world. The freedom that so many took for granted each day, my husband was giving his life to defend. So from these many examples of godly women, I learned to exhort my husband for successes and to comfort him at life's defeats. As a Christian military spouse, my role is not only to support and exhort, but to have a faith so strong and committed that others who have come behind me can imitate my faith . . . just as I have been blessed to imitate theirs.   —*Carol*

Remember your leaders, who spoke
the word of God to you. Consider the outcome
of their way of life and imitate their faith.
—Hebrews 13:7

Lord, teach me always to be strong,

To remember to Whom I belong,

To lead with faith as you would have us do,

So others will be led to You!

To exhort, uplift, and love those you put in my life,

To help them get through this journey without so much strife.

Lord, I want to be the supporter and friend

To my husband, children, and those I meet without end,

To show them the confidence of my faith with love,

That they will also be blessed from above.

Amen.

Red and Yellow, Black and White

One of the amazing teachings that happens in the military family—without their even thinking about it—is how to appreciate and love the diversity in our world.

It has been marvelous to meet people from all over the globe as we have been stationed in foreign countries. We have met students at the training schools who have come in from other nations and cultures. We have observed the customs, the costumes, the spiritual beliefs, the traditions, and the amazing beauty of all of God's creation. Our family has truly had the opportunity to get to know the heart of people—all kinds of people—and how precious we all are to our Creator.

So often in the civilian culture, people do not have the opportunity to meet others who are unlike them. They often stay in the same geographical area and grow their family and friends there. That is not a bad thing; it's just something that does not always help in the understanding of diversity.

These types of experiences are very unique to the military family. I feel they are a very important part in bringing up children, helping them to truly love with their hearts, to get to know people without any preconceived notion of what others should be like . . . or not be like.

These are the kind of people that military children become. They're also the kind of people who are able to love others with an unconditional love.

Isn't that just what Jesus did? He walked up to the Pharisees, the prostitutes, the tax collectors, or whomever—and He met them where they were. He loved them in spite of what others thought or tried to tell Him about them.

I believe that traveling and becoming culturally diverse in our experiences makes the military family a unique entity in today's society. It has made me a better Christian witness. It has made our sons well-balanced in their people skills, and has enabled us as a family to always have open arms to others within our community. I am so thankful to have had a taste of what heaven will be like someday.

—*Carol*

There is neither Jew nor Greek,
there is neither slave nor free, male nor female;
for you are all one in Christ Jesus.
—Galatians 3:28

Will there be any Baptists when we meet Him "face to face"?

Will there be any semblance of any certain race?

Will there be integration and even separate styles of song?

Or will we just be thankful and praise Him all day long?

I pray we will know the reality of Christian unity even now.

In Jesus' name. Amen.

Clinging to the Vine

Throughout my husband's military career, I have known many wives who completely dedicated themselves to military life. They served on community advisory boards, attended most social events, chaired school committees, and were involved in many of the activities that would go along with their husband's job or position. They were part of the reason why the military installations and surrounding communities functioned so well.

I know this because, while my husband was on active duty, I was one of those wives. It was a wonderful experience for me, and I met the most interesting people because of my involvement in so many different arenas. But when involvement such as this becomes the only thing we cling to, we are left with nothing when military life is over.

We recently moved to Huntsville, Alabama, and purchased a home away from the busyness of city life. We now own a couple of acres with many beautiful trees. We have several pear trees which not only grow quickly but also seem to be the first to go when storms arise.

During the last storm, I looked out our living room window and saw a huge section of one of the pear trees on the ground. I was saddened by this, because this tree provided us much shade from the summer sun. As the storm subsided, I walked out the back door and into the yard to get a closer look.

The tree looked so bare. It now revealed to predators several nests that were previously protected by its branches. There was an obvious scar on the side of the tree from the massive section that had been broken off, and the leaves on the fallen piece were already beginning to curl as they had been cut off from their life source. The only way to get this tree shaped back up would be for someone to come in the fall and drastically cut it, so it can begin growing complete and full again.

I saw in this damaged tree an important lesson: When we dedicate ourselves to a way of life instead of to Him—Who is our life—we will curl up and die by being cut off from our life source. Without Him in our lives, there is no purpose or direction.

As Jesus said, "If anyone does not abide in Me, he is thrown away as a branch, and dries up; and they gather them and cast them into the fire and they are burned" (John 15:6, NASB). When we stay plugged in to Christ as our life source, however, He allows us to see the next chapter in our lives as a part of His perfect plan. Life continues to be a godly adventure!

We can love being involved in military life, but it cannot be the driving force of our lives. We must stay connected and continue to grow in our faith and love for our Father. He will give us the strength to keep on keeping on.

Whether you are already into retirement from the military or just getting closer to that time, draw from the true source of life. Get into the Word and live with the purpose God created for you—to live to serve Him!

—*Carol*

I am the vine, you are the branches; he who abides in Me, and I in him, he bears much fruit; for apart from Me you can do nothing.
—John 15:5 (NASB)

Father, I ask that You never let me get too busy or too preoccupied with the duties of the day. Help me to look to You as the source of my life. I pray that You will give me strength and courage during times of transition. Keep me ever clinging to You, for You are the Way, the Truth, and the Life. Amen.

Training for the Real World

Do you remember the scene in the movie *Titanic* where Leonardo DiCaprio is on the front of the ship and he says, "I AM KING OF THE WORLD!" as the wind blows through his hair and the music crescendos? Well, at my husband's retirement ceremony, I felt a bit like that.

I watched as he stood in his full dress uniform with medals that had been pinned on through the years. I listened as they announced the different job assignments he had fulfilled and the accomplishments he had achieved during his time in service to our mighty nation. I was very proud of him as I was reminded of what a wonderful man he is and what incredible things he had achieved.

I also reminisced about the positions I had held during his time of active duty. I thought of the hours of volunteer time I had logged through community service opportunities, chapel activities, and school events. I remembered all of the coffees I had hosted and the functions I had led as a commander's wife. I recalled the assistance I had always given to the family support groups. I had been a great military wife, and I was very proud of what my husband and I had accomplished together in our twenty-two years of serving on active duty.

Why, we were "king and queen of the world!"

In retrospect, I truly believe that the lessons I learned and the opportunities I enjoyed as a military spouse trained me for the life that has followed. Let me mention just a few that have stood out to me and have made me better equipped for the real world.

Culturally, I have experienced so much of the world firsthand that my vision of the world has expanded well beyond my Southern upbringing. This broadening of experience has brought a greater understanding when dealing with people. This has been especially valuable when I have associated with people who have never left the same fifty-mile radius all their lives. Many people have a very narrow view of the world because they have never had the opportunity to view the world. My experiences as a military spouse have allowed me to share with others the invaluable gems that have increased my understanding.

Another way being a military spouse has prepared me for the real world is in the area of patience. Waiting accompanies military life. The military family waits for orders for the next assignment, and we wait for Dad to return after a deployment. I wish I had a dollar for every hour I stood in a commissary line . . . waiting. I have had countless opportunities to recognize that there may be a greater purpose for standing in lines than meets the eye. Times of waiting have challenged me to look at these moments as opportunities to minister. I am now able to wait in line and start a conversation or say an encouraging word to someone who looks unhappy or disgruntled.

Military life also prepared my children to face the world with greater confidence. I have watched as our sons have been through many transitions in their young adult years since their Dad's retirement. Military kids as a group are very resilient and independent. Our boys have learned how to befriend people and make the most of just about any situation. This lesson was definitely enhanced through the various traveling experiences they had. They never meet a stranger and can converse with people in all walks of life.

But one benefit of military life stands above them all—my love of America and democracy. I pray my patriotism is contagious! We live in a world that wants to question everything our president does. Many desire to make politics and polls the most important part of our American spirit. It is easy to forget that military personnel have taken an oath to protect and defend the rights of anyone in our country to express themselves—even those who have misguided opinions.

While we are in the midst of experiencing the daily activities of military life, we are not always aware that we are in preparation for the future. But God knows the plans He has for us. He wants us to be ready to share the wisdom we have gained through the years and to let others know the power of trusting Him.

Whatever stage of life you find yourself in, may the Lord bless you as you train to live in the "real world." He is an ever-present help to comfort and guide you.

—*Carol*

And we know that in all things God works for the good of those who love him, who have been called according to his purpose.
—Romans 8:28

Heavenly Father, I feel so honored to have served as a military spouse. I know that my experiences—whether they be sad or wonderful, frustrating or joyful—will all be used to Your glory if I am willing to offer them to You. Thank You for calling me to be Your child. Help me to fulfill Your purpose in my life today. In Jesus' name. Amen.

Where Now?

Okay, for those of you getting closer to the "getting out" time called retirement, don't get overconfident that you are finally going to have a chance to settle down.

In the seven years since Richard's military retirement out of Fort McPherson, Georgia, we have now moved four times! The funny thing is, since our sons graduated from high school, they have moved once a year through college and after graduation. That means they have moved seven times in seven years! Whew!!!

Does it get in one's blood to move? Maybe it does! Or does God choose certain people for military life to teach them to let go and be willing to serve wherever and whenever? I think it's a little of both. It almost seems, for our family, that the excitement and anticipation of waiting for orders to PCS during those twenty-two years of active duty deposited the itch to move in our blood.

I know that those of you who have experienced the military lifestyle up to and even into retirement understand the importance of our willingness to serve. And as Christians, we are to serve wherever we are called and to bloom where we are planted. The time of retirement is a different time of service. It is usually a time of the empty nest and getting reacquainted with each other as a couple. Whenever we move to a new place now, we are no longer Neil and Alex's mom and dad, but just Rick and Carol. It is a time when we are able to give ourselves in service to others as a couple, have friends as a couple, go to a movie or out to eat any time we want instead of being divided with children's activities.

The Bible teaches us that Jesus came to this earth as God in the flesh to experience everything we would go through. He was the son of Mary and Joseph. I am sure He was joyful, playful, loving, and kind. He learned a trade from his earthly father and sat at his feet. As he matured and the time was right, He was then recognized as God's Son, Jesus. Mary became not just Mary, but Mary, the mother of Jesus.

Even Jesus experienced different times in His life of service and ministry. His identification moved into one of much greater significance as He came to the cross, revealing Himself to be the One whom He had been all along—our Lord and Savior.

In this time of retirement, empty nest, and continual change—whether it is moving or just changing as we grow older together—I pray it will be a time that we grow deeper in our commitment to the Lord. My desire is that my husband and I become so rooted in who we are in Him that the service we give to others will be a witness to the love God has shown to us through the years!

I exhort those of you reaching these retirement years to prepare for them by praying God will not let you "check out" or get too settled in one place (even if you don't have to physically move). You have been brought to this place, filled with experiences and wisdom that will only be used when shared with others. You, my friends, have only just begun to serve in God's Army!

—*Carol*

Preach the Word! Be ready in season and out of season. Convince, rebuke, exhort, with all longsuffering and teaching.

—2 Timothy 4:2 (NASB)

I remember thinking through the years,
"Getting Out" is where it's at!
I can't wait to stay in one place;
Move again? You can forget that!

All the time not knowing
Just what God had in store,
Keeping us in one place for just a while
As He opened another door.

Now, I could really whine and cry;
Unpack boxes AGAIN? You'd hear me say.
But I have come to realize
That service to Him is the only way.

So, we will serve and continue
This second half of life together,
Knowing God is always in control,
And He will leave us never!
Amen.

How Does That Translate?

$\mathcal{I}$ remember the first interview my husband had upon retirement from twenty-two years of service in the Army. Retiring as a lieutenant colonel, he had been trained in many areas. He had experience in command positions, as second in command XO (executive officer), staff administrative positions, counseling soldiers about finances and marriages, flying attack helicopters, survival training, and being responsible for millions of dollars of equipment as well as hundreds of men and women.

He came down the stairs that morning looking so businesslike with dark suit, white shirt, and dark tie with flecks of red. He looked so handsome and self-assured. Everything he was wearing was brand-new, and I knew by that afternoon he would come home with a brand new job to begin our brand new life as civilians.

We prayed, kissed, and hugged—and off he went into corporate America.

He came back almost four hours later, walking in and saying, "They just don't get it. I have experience in every area they need. But the military experience just doesn't translate! I need to go back to square one and rewrite my resumé in civilian terms."

Here was this man, trained to protect and willing to die for not only our country and our freedom, but also, yes, for corporate America! And they didn't think his military experience translated? Hello?

My first inclination was anger—anger that there was no true appreciation of the sacrifices of military life from anyone outside the military. I thought maybe it was time to really retire. Often military retirements occur at the same time that children are going to college or planning weddings, so it is not always a financially feasible time to stop earning a paycheck. It was difficult for us to think about real retirement at that point.

Over a period of time, however, several things became evident to us both.

I watched as disappointment gave way to determination. "I can do everything through him who gives me strength" (Philippians 4:13).

Pity parties gave way to prayer. "The prayer of a righteous man is powerful and effective" (James 5:16).

Feeling alone gave way to sharing our hearts and feelings with others. "For where two or three come together in my name, there am I with them" (Matthew 18:20).

And then, defeat gave way to victory.

About eight months after that first interview—and many interviews later—my husband met with a man whose father had been in the military. Richard came home with a smile, saying, "He got it! It translated! He understands what elements I can bring to a civilian organization."

Disappointment gave way to sheer joy and confidence! We were on our way to being full-blown civilians!

"I know the plans I have for you, declares the Lord, "plans to prosper you and not to harm you, plans to give you hope and a future."
—Jeremiah 29:11

He knows the plans. He holds our future. Each of our experiences are allowed by Him and filtered through Him.

—Carol

Lord, forgive me that I think of Your plans for us as disappointments. Forgive me for not realizing that the stumbling blocks we encounter are often used as stepping stones to draw us closer to You. Father, thank You for honoring my husband with civilian jobs so that he can be a blessing and bring to others the expertise he has acquired while in military service. Praise You, Lord, for all these things. In Jesus' name. Amen.

Looking Ahead

We are being perfected until the day of Christ Jesus.

I have taken such comfort in the fact that I am being perfected in the future tense. I am so thankful I have not stayed in a place of staleness and sin.

I can always look ahead and know there is a new and often better day coming.

A couple of things that I dealt with in our early marriage have had to be perfected in me: jealousy and fear.

I was so jealous of anyone showing attention to my husband. He is a very handsome man, and to me, any attention shown to him by others carried innuendo. I know now, of course, that this was my insecurity and immaturity and had nothing to do with him or anyone else.

I dealt with fear when we were separated. I feared some-one harming the children or me while Richard was away in the field. I feared the boys getting sick. (I spent many hours in Germany at the Hanau Clinic in the middle of the night when Richard was on eight weeks of military exercise.) I continually feared that our sons might die when they were young.

Jealousy and fear are two of the enemy's ugly heads! They were stealing my joy and taking away any witness from my Christian walk, which was very weak at the time.

I would never have realized in looking ahead that I would come to a place of such love and adoration for my husband that I would want people to pay attention to him. It is amazing to think that I would come to a point—as I am being perfected—of knowing who I am in Christ and being confident in my marriage.

This perfection process has also been aided through the mentoring and direction of a sister in Christ, by going to my knees and praying to give our sons and our lives to the Lord. Knowing He loves them so much more than I do and that they will be on earth or with Him has brought such comfort, love, and absence of fear.

Looking ahead, I am excited about continuing to share my life with the husband of my youth. I look forward to daughters-in-law, to grandchildren and, yes, to great-grandchildren.

I look forward to the plans God has for us—plans for a future and a hope. When troubles come, I know we are being perfected to face them with prayer and confidence, and that if anyone is in control, God is!

Looking ahead? I just know that everything with God is future tense until He comes back for His Bride or until we meet Him at the end of our lives.

—*Carol*

. . . being confident of this, that he who began a good work in you will carry it on to completion until the day of Christ Jesus.

—Philippians 1:6

Dear Lord, I am so imperfect at this stage of my life. Just when I think I have the answer, the question changes. Just when I think that everything is going pretty well, another challenge is presented to get me on my face before You. Help me to help You work out the "good work" in me. Help my willingness to listen and learn be ever increased as time goes by. Amen.

Acknowledgements

For both of us, the writing of this book is a culmination of divine appointments with many people, beginning with our meeting one another many years ago. We are so thankful that the Lord allowed our paths to cross and continued to intersect those paths through circumstances only He could orchestrate. The sharing of our dreams and gifts has been most rewarding.

This book is a collection of stories about a lifestyle that we both have loved. Along the way, we have encountered people who have been part of the stories and have encouraged the telling of them.

We thank Sam for your patriotism and for recognizing the need for such a book as this.

We thank Bruce for being the best JAG ever.

We thank the Broadman and Holman family for hearing our hearts and recognizing a need to affirm and support military families. Thanks to Lawrence Kimbrough for being our advocate and our guide through this process. Lawrence, you have always had a "smile"—even over the phone—and have been an amazing source of help.

From Carol—

Thank you, Mother and Dad, for always praying us through each move and transition. We will always have such wonderful memories of your visits to every new assignment.

Thank you, McGlothlin family, for sharing room and board and lots of cookouts during our times of travel.

Thank you to my sister, Vicki. I always felt we had truly been on a family vacation after visiting with you in Tennessee.

Thank you to my Christian brothers and sisters who have prayed for me and exhorted me to keep going at each turn of this project.

From Brenda—

Thanks, Glen and Ruth, for telling me long ago that this could happen.

Thanks, Karen, for cheering me on.

Thanks to all my PWOC sisters, who truly are my "sisters."

Thanks, Dad, for your love of books and the disciplined life you have led before me. I appreciate the encouragement and prayers you and Mom have always provided.

Thanks to my Pace family for the blessing you are in my life.

Thanks, Megan, for being a wonderful daughter-in-law, and for the joy that you, Jolie, and Noah have brought to us.

From both of us —

We are both blessed to have wonderful sons in Neil and Alex (Carol) and Gregory and Joseph (Brenda). Boys, as our families traveled around the world, you have become anything but military "brats." We are grateful for the fine young men you are. Thanks for making us laugh and being so flexible as we moved you from pillar to post.

And finally, we want to thank our husbands—the two Richards—for the adventure of a lifetime. Your love of God and country through your service in the U.S. Armed Forces has been inspiring and contagious. You are deeply loved and respected by us, and we thank you for allowing us to accompany you on this journey that has drawn us closer as a family and closer to our Lord. This year we both celebrate thirty years of marriage, and the adventure continues! You are our heroes!

Brenda and Carol would love to hear from you!
Please contact them at medalsaboveheart@aol.com
Let them know how this book has encouraged you.

You are also invited to send your own story of how life in the military has been a rewarding experience for you, to be possibly included in a future publication. To inquire about speaking engagements with Brenda and/or Carol at your church or event, please contact them at the above e-mail address.